MW01602725

101 WAYS

to create a

CHIC

and

charming

HOME

Everything you need to know
to turn your space into
your dream home

CHIARA GIULIANI

101 Ways to Create
A Chic and Charming
Home

Everything You Need to Know
to Turn Your Space
into Your Dream Home

Chiara Giuliani

ENGLISH EDITION
EDITED BY
ELITE AUTHORS

Text © 2023 Chiara Giuliani

Book cover design © 2023 by Emily's World of Design.
All rights reserved.

Illustrations:
Chapters 15, 27, 31, 38, 56, 90 © Pamon Chopudsa/Shutterstock.com, Chapters 19, 24 © PaoloGenoa/Shutterstock.com, Chapters 20, 22, 29, 33, 44, 51, 64, 75 © Interior Design/Shutterstock.com, Chapters 23, 25 © Alesandro14/Shutterstock.com, Chapter 39 © CastecoDesign/Shutterstock.com, Chapters 45, 47, 62 © Katunina/Shutterstock.com, Chapter 87 © AVD_88/Shutterstock.com, Chapter 9 3 © Kamieshkova/Shutterstock.com, Chapter 96 © Beyond Time/Shutterstock.com, Chapter 98 © DoubleBubble/Shutterstock.com, page 76 © Olillia/Shutterstock.com

All rights reserved.

All rights reserved. This book or any portion thereof may not be reproduced or used in any manner whatsoever without the express written permission of the publisher except for the use of brief quotations in a book review.

ISBN: 9798862488517

www.ladonnadicharme.com

Also by Chiara Giuliani
Winner of the Corporate Vision 2023 Global Business Award as "Style and Fashion Expert of the Year 2023"

101 Ways to Look Expensive on a Budget
Everything You Need to Know
To Become the Classiest Lady Ever

101 Ways to Become Your Best Chic Self
Everything You Need to Know
To Unlock the Princess in You

101 Ways to Look Slimmer and Taller
How to Lengthen Your Body
and Get a Taller-Appearing Figure

Flattering Fashion
How to Turn Trends to Your Advantage,
Enhancing Your Figure, And Achieving a Sensational Style

The Fashion Diet
Lower Your Weight While Uplifting Your Mood

Wardrobe Essentials for a Woman of Charme
A Timeless Guide to Looking Slim and Chic

How to Become a Woman of Charme
The Ultimate Guide to Timeless Style

Ladonnadicharme

Style & Fashion Expert of the Year 2023 - Italy

To my parents,
who taught me with love
what a charming and chic home is.

Table of Contents

Preface

Styling your home is a bit like choosing a dress—and maybe it's also for this reason that we ladies love it so much.

An appropriate dress can make you feel better, more attractive, and in a better mood. Also, it can help you minimize challenging areas while enhancing your assets.

Exactly in the same way, **decoration and furniture can modify a room and make the most of its potential exactly as makeup, grooming, and clothes can change your look and make you feel happier with yourself.**

As Coco Chanel once stated (and as I like to quote in many of my writings), "Fashion is architecture: it's a matter of proportion." And the opposite is also valid, which means that styling your place may have the same impact on your mood as taking appropriate care of your persona.

Spending some time to improve your home and to boost its potential, and **making some little but effective changes to its decoration and organization**, can do wonders to make it look more beautiful and welcoming, and—most importantly—**to make you feel better and put you in a better mood.**

An oh-so-me home not only is more enjoyable, but it's also easier to manage.

And even if, when it comes to decorating, styling, and organizing your space, things can sometimes seem overwhelming, **with the appropriate mindset and some useful hints, you will find it a fun and fulfilling activity**.

In this guide, you will learn **easy and inexpensive tricks to make your home your chic place**, but you'll also find more than that.

You will acquire the **technical expertise to make your place look bigger, brighter, and more enjoyable**, together with the practical know-how to manage it in the most effective way.

You will learn **easy but effective styling tips** and useful advice to organize your spaces, making them look more orderly with no effort.

You will also find practical guidelines. The most technical ones have been streamlined for you in the easiest possible way. As for the most aesthetic rules, they are explained so that they can be fun and become—if you want—an occasion to spend some quality time with your dear ones.

Not only will you learn **the secrets to creating a place that infuses you with energy** (instead of just taking energy away to tidy it), but you will also soon acquire the skills to **transform your home from just ordinary to classy in no time**, thus making your setting pleasant, soothing, relaxing, and welcoming with quite a low investment.

The guidelines that you will learn are suitable whether your goal is a luxurious, expensive-looking place or an intimate, cozy, down-to-earth environment.

Whether you are considering just some minor changes or are in the mood for a big transformation, in all cases, you will find rules and principles that will guide you in the choice of, for example, a lamp, as well as in deciding the pattern, material, and color of wall tiles, or choosing a big furniture piece.

With the help of the abovementioned technical and esthetical tools, you will soon **develop practical know-how and effortlessly enhance your innate good taste**.

Your home will become more and more beautiful and enjoyable over the years.

And you will soon create **a place where you can feel glad, positive, and successful, boosting and enjoying that chic vibe** that's so appropriate for the chic and charming lady that you already are.

Introduction

Many people asked me to translate my first book, *La Casa di Charme*, from Italian into English. This is the book everything comes from, I'd say (meaning all my following books and manuals). In fact, it was after the publication of that down-to-earth home-style manual—and after receiving so many nice messages from my lovely readers—that I figured out that I could go on and write something similar regarding personal style and lifestyle as well.

However, its translation is easier said than done.

That guide was specifically written for Italy - which means that it contains a good number of tips to give style to places that were originally styled centuries ago and to manage workers who are not very inclined to be managed.

Though, since the main guidelines to turn your space into your dream place are somehow transversal to most local customs, I decided that I could still pick out the most effective hints that I wrote in that first guide, turning them into a small manual easy to read, simple to understand, and fun to put into practice.

The result is the mini-book that now you're holding, which is, at the same time:

- A little guide in which I share with you **some unsaid truths** that will make you understand **why so many houses lack the appropriate atmosphere, even if lots of money was spent** on their decoration and furniture.

- A manual with **practical hints and tips to manage your home with little effort**, making it more enjoyable and easy to handle with just some small but impactful changes.

- A handbook with **the main secrets to turning an ordinary place into a stylish and charming home** that makes you feel glad, relaxed, and fulfilled in every moment of your day.

This short guide—like its elder sister—has the main objective of helping my stylish readers **achieve the best home goals in no time, without spending a lot of money, and without having to call professionals**.

Unlike most books about interior design, you won't need to have technical skills, have graduated in construction projects, or have a degree in plant engineering to understand its content.

We will cover together the most important steps in the (sometimes) tricky but always fulfilling path of organizing and restyling your domestic spaces.

You will learn that **having a home that's chic and sophisticated**, a home of timeless *charme*,[1] **is not a matter of money**. You don't need to have a limitless budget and limitless time to achieve it—**just your good taste, the appropriate**

---

[1] *Charme* is a French word whose meaning is slightly different from the English word *charm* and indicates "an ensemble of beauty, elegance, appeal, allure, and style."

organization and mood, plus some technical and aesthetic skills that you can learn with ease and fun.

And you will soon realize how, even if it sounds surprising, **living in a beautiful, well-organized setting is a powerful tool to make you feel successful**, thus boosting your self-esteem.

Not only will you have the beautiful home you desire, but this will make you feel more positive and self-confident as well.

I hope that you will enjoy the road that we are going to cover together.

Just follow the path.

And the results, believe me, will be exciting!

Part 1

Identifying Your Home

Identifying Your Home

1. As mentioned in the preface, a home is like a dress. You don't need to have the most expensive, the most elegant, or the latest trend. Rather, you should always **pick out the one that makes you feel good, that fits you better, and that's in tune with your style, lifestyle, and personality**—and this is what you are going to learn with this little manual.

2. To start with, it may be useful to **focus on your priorities in a conscious way** and to set what we can call your main "home goals." Do you want a place that's easier to manage on a daily basis? Or is it more important to have a space that's warm and welcoming when you have guests? Maybe you would like to have a bedroom that's more intimate and relaxing to enjoy some quality time with your partner in a soothing setting. Or you've just had a baby and want everything to be safe for him or her to explore the world. **Concentrate on what is most important for you and your family.** Once you decide the main direction to take, the rest will flow quite easily.

3. To succeed in your home-styling journey without ending up overwhelmed in a sea of to-do lists, I suggest that you **start with one room at a time or—even better—one corner at a time**. It can be the living room, if you have frequent gatherings and like to have friends around. It can be the

bedroom, if your main goal is having a cozy place to share with your partner. Or it may also be the bathroom, if you need a place for yourself to enjoy self-care and get that extra energy that you need to manage your daily tasks. **Focusing on just one area at a time** will allow you to experiment in quite an easy way. You will **achieve results that can be visible almost immediately, to have extra motivation to go on and do a good job** with the rest of the house.

4. As usual, **cultivating good taste is essential** when it comes to making your place your dream place. **This is a fun activity**, and if you can **arrange it to engage the whole family**, you already have in your hands the key to creating a unique and tailor-made setting. From time to time, schedule a visit to a local museum, or visit an art gallery. And when you're traveling, ask your dear ones (your partner, your friends, or your kids) to look around and describe what they like in the surrounding landscape—and why. **You don't need to go to a national park or visit the most impressive monuments** to do this. **It may also be something simple as looking at the patterns of the clouds in the sky** or the harmony of the colors of the trees. It's a lovely way to spend some quality time together, and it will serve to refine your taste and give you a sophisticated sensibility. This will contribute to defining a place that's enjoyable and fulfilling and makes you feel at home in its deeper meaning.

5. Consider that **in home decor, there are trends** exactly as there are with garments. What's different is that **we are seldom aware of them**. Therefore, we may unconsciously make choices that have nothing to do with our real taste, lifestyle, and personality but that are mere consequences of what we see around us. This entirely backfires, of course, since it can lead us to purchase things that we won't easily hide in a drawer when the trend has passed (not to mention the fact that a sofa usually has a price that's considerably higher than that of a skirt). However, the good news is that the **good taste mentioned in the previous point is a**

matchless tool to skip this obstacle since it will always allow you to recognize a trend that's tasteful and classy rather than an untasteful fad.

6. Also, **it may be useful to be aware of where decoration trends come from** in order to perceive them properly from the beginning. As mentioned above, unlike clothing fashion, vogues related to decoration and furniture usually do not arrive to us directly. They come in more subtle, less detectable forms. We can find them in TV programs and movies, but also in commercials for completely different kinds of products. **Social media** also **contributes to unconsciously suggesting to the brain the image of an ideal setting**. This image settles into our subconscious, and when we recognize it around us, we feel a sensation of coziness—not necessarily because what we see is in tune with our mindset and habits, but because we have seen it so many times without even perceiving it. Therefore, **a useful exercise is trying to detect in a mindful way what's in vogue for domestic settings**. This is essential to be aware of trends and fads: not to avoid them altogether (they can be a useful inspiration), but rather, to avoid making choices that, when seen closely, may be not that suitable to your lifestyle—and to your deeper *you*.

7. **Always consider that trends are a tool**. And the only chic way to handle them is **taking advantage of the vogues, instead of merely accepting what they suggest**. Luckily enough, **from 2020 on, most trends in home styling are quite tasteful**—as if the pandemic gave rise to styles that are chic and, in general, classier than the average, in order to make staying at home more pleasant. However, this was not always the case. I remember that when I set up my first home, a horrible shade of reddish wood was all the rage for furniture, together with huge shelves that made the widest of places look smaller than a storage room. **Making the most of trends and filtering them with your good taste** will help you get through questionable fads. This way, your home will

become your unique, charming place, and it will always be **trendy and super stylish while still expressing your own style and personality.**

8. Exactly as with garments, **it's more important to consider the whole effect than the individual pieces.** And as always, **proportion among the different elements is the key** to achieving outstanding results. Proportions in colors, shapes, patterns, and styles are essential to creating a lovely setting, as we will see in detail in the next chapters. But also, there should be proportions between your settings, your lifestyle, and your priorities in life. **Be realistic** about them. And don't buy that super expensive sofa covered in luxurious velvet if you like to relax in your living room painting your toes on the couch every other day.

9. **Choose your style and follow what your deeper self suggests, but be open-minded.** You can always find an approach (or maybe just a decor piece) that you had never considered before but that's in tune with your mindset, taste, and lifestyle. **This is most important since the choices related to your home should also consider the opinions of your dear ones**, which may not coincide with yours. Therefore, **brainstorming and window-shopping instead of arguing and making impulsive purchases** is always the most effective way to create a space where you really feel at home. This way, you may come across something that may be surprisingly in tune with your mood. And this will lead to something that's considerably more valuable (also in terms of family relationships) than what you would have chosen in the beginning.

10. **Have fun experimenting.** Unsure about what the most appropriate dimension for your coffee table may be? Take a big piece of thick cardboard and cut from it a shape of dimensions identical to the hypothetical item that you would like to buy. Place the shape over a support base (some books can also do the job), and put it in the desired spot. Leave it

there for some time; you will soon realize if it's too big or too small, and if the position is the most appropriate. Or **use an inflatable sofa for some time if you can't decide on the shape and color of the real one**. This way, you won't buy (and spend money) in a hurry, and your choices will always be the most well-considered ones. I personally did this for many pieces in my first home, and it was such a lot of fun! We had the "fake" furniture around for months in some cases. And the results were entirely fulfilling from any point of view.

11. As I frequently underline in my writings, **always make searching (instead of purchasing) become a pleasure**. This is a very sophisticated skill. Aside from being fun, **it will allow you to develop style skills, save money**, and achieve the final reward: a home that fits you in the deepest way.

12. Be aware that even if an item has a high price, this does not necessarily mean that it's chic. **Class and style frequently have nothing to do with price.** Always look for **harmony and proportion**, since they are **the only keys to achieving a classy, welcoming, and cozy home**. And they will give your place that extra touch that will make it unique.

Part 2

Enhancing the Hardware:

Colors and Materials

Enhancing the Hardware: Colors and Materials

Choosing and Pairing Colors

13. **If you want to create a home that's chic, stylish, and enjoyable**, one of the main cornerstones is **an appropriate choice of colors**. Just changing the color on one or two walls and switching a couple of throw pillows with others in a more appropriate hue can have as a result an entirely different (and much chicer) vibe. It can boost beautiful things and minimize possible faults. And interestingly, **what's important is not the color in itself, but the overall effect of the different shades together**. And it's **their harmony (or the lack of it) that makes the difference** between just an ordinary room and a charming, welcoming place.

14. Whatever the scale and dimensions, an appropriate color choice is the tool No. 1 to have outstanding results and to create the home of your dreams. Learning the secrets to managing the countless hues of each color and becoming able to handle them is the key to any chic setting. **A suitable color can add class and style to a room much more than any expensive piece**. And even if this may sound surprising to some, it's really not, because **the color is the first feature we perceive of a given item - whereas its exact shape requires a longer time to be clearly perceived**. Not only

will a proper color choice elevate your place from common to stylish, but **it will also make you feel good in every moment of your day**, giving you energy when you need a boost or making you feel soothed when you need to relax.

15. To better understand the importance of chromatic harmony, imagine one of those perfectly styled rooms that you see in magazines or online, and imagine just changing a detail. For instance, in a room in the shades of sand, ivory, and off-white, with walls in a deep shade of dusty blue (as in the picture below), imagine adding an item in a brilliant tone of pink. Not only will this remove all the allure of that soothing atmosphere, but it will also make the place look smaller, removing class and style from previously stylish pieces. The same would happen if, in a space where intense tones prevail, you add something in a faint hue. **It is not a matter of a specific color**. Rather, as always, **the result is given by the appropriate combination of the different elements**. Brilliant or subdued hues can produce exactly the same breathtaking results, as long as there is **chromatic coherence**.

16. Also, consider that, interestingly, not only will an appropriate color choice allow you to create stylish settings, but (this may sound unexpected) **it will also lead to a home that's easier to maintain since it will make the place look more polished and organized** in the bargain. The good news is that choosing the most suitable color ensemble for a room is not that different from the choice of the color ensemble for your daily outfits. Just increase the dimensions, and you're done.

17. There are many **different approaches to color choice**, some of which may look quite cumbersome. Talking from personal experience, I found that the easiest method is the **HSV model**, a system used for classifying colors.

    It consists of identifying:

    the main **hue (H)**, which indicates **the pure color** being referenced, meaning red, yellow, blue, and so on;

    its **saturation (S)**, which refers to **how much white has been added to the base color** (if the saturation is total, meaning that it's devoid of white, the color is pure, whereas if white is gradually added, the color becomes fainter);

    its brightness or **value (V)**, meaning **the amount of black that has been added** to the color.

    From the sum of the previous items, we can then obtain countless **shades**, which **are the results of adding gray (white + black) to the original hue**. The addition of gray transforms a hue into its neutral version—that is, a **tonality where the original color is somehow toned down**, as you can see in the picture below. For instance, tan is a neutral shade of yellow that has quite a high saturation (it contains just a small dose of white) and quite a low value (it contains a good dose of black). Sand is another neutral shade of yellow that, conversely, has quite low saturation (since there is a lot of white in it) and quite a high brightness/value (as it contains just a small quantity of black).

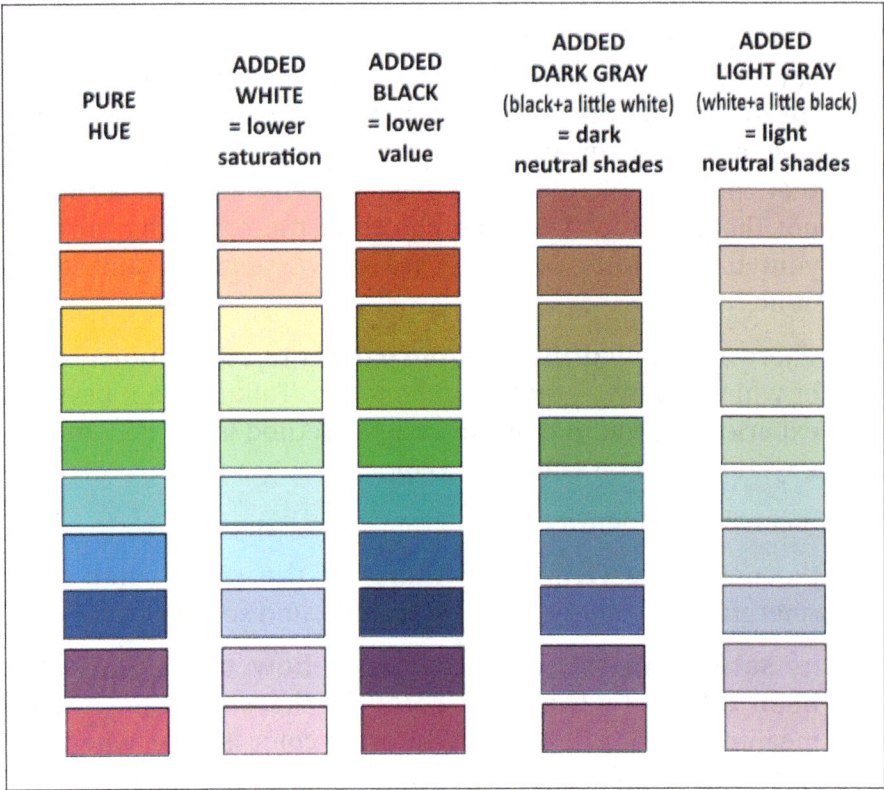

PURE HUE	ADDED WHITE = lower saturation	ADDED BLACK = lower value	ADDED DARK GRAY (black+a little white) = dark neutral shades	ADDED LIGHT GRAY (white+a little black) = light neutral shades

18. **Once you have detected the three main features of a given color**, you can choose to **pair it**: (a) with **hues that have a similar saturation**, (b) with **tints that have a similar value,** or (c) with **tones of the same shade—***even if they come from a completely different hue.* For instance, dusty green and rose taupe (which you can find in the table above, in the column of light neutral shades), even if originating from entirely different hues (green and red), create a very sophisticated ensemble, since their harmony comes from the fact that they have a similar intensity. The same can be said, for instance, for ivory and pearl; for carbon gray and syrup; for cognac and charcoal; and of course, for countless others. Since the original tone is attenuated, **shades can easily match with any other tone, allowing chic and**

sophisticated combinations. Contrary to common opinion, neutrals do not include only faded colors but also intense tints. Finding the most sophisticated pairings, aside from being lots of fun, can become a useful way to deepen your aesthetic skills and your good taste.

19. **Alternating cool neutral hues and warm neutral ones** will give your home a sophisticated appearance that is elegant while in the meantime making everybody feel at ease. **This pairing is perfect for light colors as well as for dark ones.** For instance, with walls and tiles in a cool neutral tone (such as gray, dusty blue, or dusty green), furniture in a warm shade of brown will have a super chic outcome, as you can see in the image below. The same is valid also for neutral light colors such as pearl (cool neutral hue) and oatmeal (warm neutral hue), for instance.

20. You can also pair different tones of the same hue using colors that remain in the same family without being identical. This is a classic color combination that, when properly applied, can

be useful to make spaces look bigger. However, consider that **when the hues are too similar, the outcome can sometimes look boring** or uninteresting. Add some detail in a complementary color (meaning the color that lies on the opposite side of the color wheel, as shown in the image on page 41) or in the corresponding warm/cool shade (as in the image below, where a mustard armchair has been added to a space in different shades of gray) **to create focal points and give spice to the place**. Also, **variations in dark and light** are perfect to add personality to your environment, making it look more interesting.

21. Still uncertain about what a proper color combination means? **Browse the web, looking for antique paintings** (from wall decorations of ancient Rome to Botticelli's *The Birth of Venus*), **and take inspiration from the color pairings that you see in them**. You won't miss a shot.

22. **White is always a perfect choice for doors, windows, frames, and details** (as long as the walls are not also painted white, of course). It makes the setting look chic and

sophisticated, adding class and style, even with inexpensive pieces. **This works with walls painted in any kind of hue.** Light shades, as well as intense and vivid tones, or dark ones, are always enhanced by elements in white since **white makes any other color look more definite**, adding personality to your home.

23. Interestingly, **white is not the most suitable color if the light is scarce**. Even if it is correctly considered the brightest color of all (since it reflects the light more than any other shade), **when there is not enough light, white becomes gray for an optical effect**. Therefore, it does not make the place appear brighter but, conversely, grayish. **As an alternative, you can use intense warm tones** (as in the image below) because these shades can give the impression that sunrays are entering the room. **Subdued hues can be another option, as long as you alternate shades that are darker and lighter**. Since the color is given by the light,

when the light is scarce, the difference between similar colors is more difficult to detect. Therefore, in this case, hues that are all the same shade (which, in bright rooms, may have a very sophisticated effect) will have an uninteresting and quite dull outcome.

24. **White is a perfect choice for painting ceilings that have a regular height** (about nine feet or lower), since it has the visual effect of amplifying the space. You may also add a strip of about one to four inches painted equally in white in the upper part of the walls. This will make the room look even bigger.

25. **When the ceilings are too high, the most suitable choice is to opt for a shade that is darker** than that of the walls. Also in this case, adding a stripe in the same color as the ceiling (or darker, as in the image below) alongside the whole perimeter of the room will make the place look more proportional and welcoming.

26. **Stark contrasts** (such as all-dark-colored furniture on all-light-colored walls and floor) can be **tricky to use when the space is not very wide, because they can make a room look smaller**. If you love stark contrasts, an easy way to use them is to choose white kitchen furniture to be positioned on a dark wall, and a similarly dark floor completed with a top in a shade similar to that of the floor. A similar ensemble, though, requires that the room is perfectly organized, with just a minimal quantity of items around. Otherwise, it will immediately give the sensation of a messy, chaotic place.

27. Don't forget that **white and its variations—such as oatmeal, beige, butter, sand, and so on—need to be**

balanced out by something darker, even if only slightly (brown, tan, camel, cognac, and caramel, for instance, are perfect, as well as darker shades such as gray or charcoal), as shown in the image below.

28. Conversely, **dark shades need to be balanced out with vivid (or intense) tones**. Bold-colored pieces and items in vivid colors add energy and light to a place where dark shades prevail. You can also achieve a similar effect using metallic hues. This will provide an outcome that's **stylish and sophisticated and that will always look classy, whatever the current trends are**.

29. As for the pairings between the furniture and the structural parts of the house (walls, floor, doors, windows), the most appropriate choices are usually the following: (a) **when the structural elements are light-colored**, the classiest choice is giving preference to **furniture that remains in the range**

of light hues but is a little lighter or a little darker than the colors of floors and walls; or (b) **when the main elements are dark-colored**, you will achieve a **stylish outcome with pieces in a color that complement them**. This means that if the main elements are in a cold shade, the furniture should be in warm hues (as in the picture below), whereas if walls and floors are warm-colored, the most stylish choice is furniture in cool tones. The abovementioned pairings, aside from being very chic, **will also make the space look welcoming, bigger, and more orderly**.

Choosing and Pairing Materials

30. If you want a home that's welcoming and stylish, **always avoid excessive matching**. This rule applies to colors as well as to patterns. Excessive matching **will give a place the appearance of having been bought on stock in a store**, instead of being the expression of the people who live in it. And this, aside from being the opposite of chic, is also the opposite of welcoming. Regarding colors, instead of repeating

the same identical hue, it's wiser **to match shades that are similar without being identical**, as demonstrated in the previous pages. Likewise, never buy a complete series of furniture all the same pattern and style. They can be of the same material but a little different in pattern, or in materials that remain in the same family. This way, you will achieve a tailored-looking and sophisticated outcome that will give class and personality to your home.

31. A classy result can also be accomplished by **playing with different scales of the same pattern or material**. Throw pillows in a fishbone pattern, for instance, are perfect for a sofa in a solid color that's paired with armchairs covered in a fishbone fabric (where the fishbone has a scale bigger than that of the throw pillows). **Scale and proportion are always the keys to a place that's stylish and sophisticated** but, at the same time, is personal and welcoming.

32. **The sofa and armchairs don't need to match**. You can achieve stunning effects by pairing pieces that have different patterns and colors (as in the picture above). Conversely, the **chairs around a table should always match not only for pattern and material but also for color**. Sure, there is a recent trend that suggests using chairs all different in colors, as well as in styles and materials, as a way to promote and implement the reuse of old furniture, but speaking from personal experience, I think it's appropriate only for a very small percentage of rural dwellings. In all other cases, it's seldom stylish. There are many other ways to use old furniture with lovely results. Skip to point 39 for details!

33. When it comes to choosing the most appropriate **materials and hues for your bedroom**, always keep in mind that, whatever style you choose for your home, the room where you sleep is a particular space. Therefore, it's better to **avoid hues that are too bright as well as contrasting tints and materials**. Even if, in the rest of the house, you used brilliant colors, cutting-edge materials, and out-of-the-ordinary patterns, **in the sleeping area, everything needs to be smooth**.

It will guarantee a stress-free bedtime, relaxing sleep, and a calm wake-up. This is essential, even if you usually like to have a very lively setting all around you. Vivid colors impact your brain in a deep, unconscious way, and it's better not to have them around just before sleeping or when waking up. Rather, give preference to shades that have quite a deep intensity in any color you like.

34. In general, you will achieve a very stylish outcome by giving preference to **natural materials such as wood, rattan, stone, and leather**, since they always give spaces a classy and welcoming vibe. Leather and suede (also synthetic) in particular are perfect for a cozy, relaxing atmosphere. Conversely, when it comes to furniture, **metal, and glass, even if perfect for structural elements, should be used only for small surfaces** or decorative pieces (as we will see in detail in part 3 of the book) because, when used for pieces of big dimensions, they can have an impersonal effect.

35. **An exception, though, are glass tabletops** since, for an optical effect, **they make the space look wider and are usually very chic**. However, this only works if the glass is transparent, as the reflection is higher, and so is the sensation of space. Avoid frosty or acid-etched glasses because not only is the widening effect considerably lower, but they are also too impersonal and are, therefore, more appropriate for professional settings (or for bathrooms).

36. **For kids' rooms**, purchasing matchy-matchy furniture, where all the pieces are the same shade and pattern, is the opposite of stylish. Besides, it won't allow the children to develop personality and good taste. **Buy just a few quality pieces (bed, desk, and closet) in timeless materials and colors, then have fun changing the rest** (chairs, chest of drawers, and all accessory pieces) as they grow. You will have **a flexible and adaptable space that you can style together**.

37. Always keep in mind that **furniture with overly trendy features is not the wisest choice since, ironically enough,**

it will soon make your home look dated. As mentioned at the beginning of the book, fashion trends in home design are much more challenging than they are for garments. Aside from the higher cost that furniture clearly has (which would imply giving preference to pieces that will likely last for many years), consider that, if you can easily store an out-of-date garment in a corner of your closet, you can hardly do the same with an outdated sofa.

38. Rather, if you would like to have in your setting a piece that's striking and eye-catching, **take something that you like just for itself—because of its uncommon shape, material, or color—not because it's trendy**. This way, there's no risk of having something that clearly shows the mark of a past trend. And you will surely like it for a long time.

39. **Vintage furniture** is an interesting and environmentally friendly way to give new life to items from the past, be they recent or not. A vintage cupboard can make an ordinary

hallway look immediately more welcoming. And an old side table can give a sophisticated and tailored vibe to your bedroom. Only, keep in mind that **when it comes to old pieces, the choice should mainly rely on tables, coffee tables**, cabinets, chest of drawers, cupboards, and, **in general, furniture that you use to *store*, not to *sit* on**. When it comes to seats, pieces from the past frequently do not offer the necessary comfort—which, with frequent use, could also cause back pain. Therefore, **for sofas, armchairs, chairs**, and, in general, seats to be used daily, **give preference to items produced with contemporary techniques and materials**. If you love antique seats, you can still use a couple of them as decorative pieces. This will add a sophisticated touch to your place without adding trouble to your bones.

40. You can find old furniture for a few bucks in thrift stores and even, sometimes, for free if you pick it up directly from the houses of the previous owners (this is valid mostly for furniture of quite big dimensions, though). **Going in search of the perfect piece can be lots of fun**. And **repainting it** not only will give you a unique piece, but it's also **something exciting to do with family and friends on a windy Sunday afternoon**.

41. Concerning repainting, an option I like very much is so-called **distressed furniture**. It consists of painting old furniture by layering two different colors, interposing a layer of wax between them, and then taking some sandpaper to remove the most superficial color on certain points, thus leaving the lower color visible (if you want to use just one color, when the top coat is sanded away, it will show the base material, usually wood). Aside from being so nice to see, **this technique is particularly appropriate for beginners, since any irregularity in the color will be perceived as a desired effect**—not as proof that you don't have any painting skills. For an all-over distressed look, take some medium grit sandpaper and rub it all over until the wood starts to show through. Aside from giving the item **a charming ancient vibe that's very French**, you can also use this technique to **change the colors of pieces that are not the most appropriate shades for your settings**, thus achieving **a tailored and very chic outcome**.

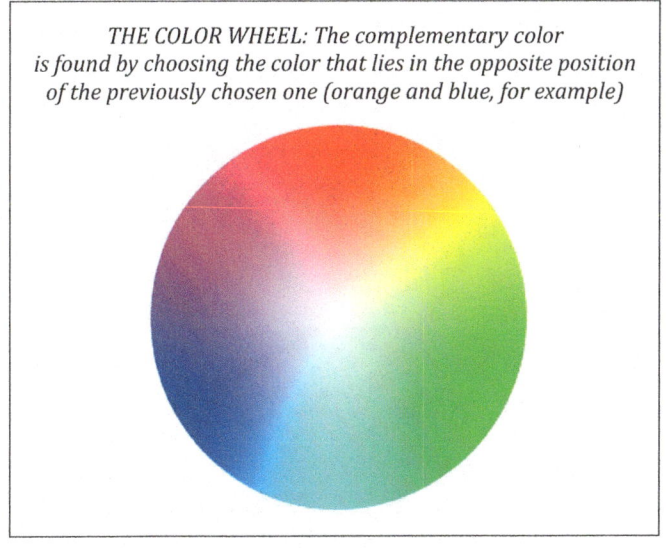

THE COLOR WHEEL: The complementary color is found by choosing the color that lies in the opposite position of the previously chosen one (orange and blue, for example)

Part 3

Boosting the Accessories:

Lighting, Paintings and Mirrors, Fabrics, and Decorative Objects

Boosting the Accessories:
Lighting, Paintings and Mirrors, Fabrics, and Decorative Objects

Lighting

42. When it comes to making your place cozy and welcoming, the **appropriate placement of lamps and lighting plays a key role,** together (this may sound surprising) with the correct choice of items to place near lamps. Also, and interestingly, consider that **when choosing a lamp, the main thing to consider is not** *the lamp's own* **appearance**. What's essential, **rather, is the appearance the lamp gives to what is** *around* **it—including people.** This is great news, since it means that you can have outstanding results even with less expensive items. Lampshades made of cloth, fabric, or even plastic usually give the room a warm atmosphere. Conversely, glass (which is frequently more expensive) may have a worse and cooler outcome.

43. Another key element to creating a relaxing atmosphere is **swapping cold light bulbs** (if there are any in your home) **with warm light ones**. To see if a bulb has a warm or cool light, **check the color temperature written on the packaging or on the bulb itself.** *(Note: Color temperature describes the light appearance provided by a light bulb. It is measured in degrees of Kelvin (K) on a scale from 1,000 to 10,000.)*

Warm-color temperatures (3000K and lower) are more appropriate for relaxing and therefore are suitable for domestic settings. Conversely, lamps with a higher color temperature ((3500K–3700K or higher) have a cool appearance and are more appropriate for work environments, since they are closer to blue and are useful when you need to focus. Color temperatures from 3000 to 3500K are considered neutral, and their effect may be influenced by the colors of walls and furniture.

44. To create a welcoming atmosphere, keep in mind that **table lamps, floor lamps, and, in general, freestanding luminaire should always be preferred over ceiling lights**. This is because when lights are placed in a low position (from the floor to about six feet), the room looks warmer—and people look more attractive in the bargain. Conversely, **when the light comes from above your head** (as is the case with most ceiling lights), **the setting looks less pleasant**. Not to mention the fact that face imperfections are highlighted, wrinkles look deeper, and eye bags appear darker—not a very satisfying outcome indeed!

45. **If you already have ceiling lamps above your dinner table**, you can simply **lower them to a height of about six**

feet from the floor. Since they are above the table, there's no risk of people banging their heads on them. For other ceiling lights, try to turn them on only when you need to have more vivid light. As substitutes, add in the room a good number of table lamps or floor lamps.

46. **Wall sconces can have a lovely outcome**—as long as they are positioned at about six feet from the floor, as mentioned in the previous points. And if you **hang framed pictures or small paintings just below them**, this will instantly make the room chic and welcoming in an intimate but stylish way.

47. Turning now to **table lamps and floor lamps**, you may **amplify their sophisticated touch by placing them in front of a mirror**. Not only will this double the light, but it will instantly make the room look warm and classy. To make the atmosphere even more stylish, **below table lamps, you may place a couple of items made of metal or glass** (a silver or steel tray, a crystal vase, or a decorative sphere). Interestingly, metal and glass, which may have a cold effect when used for furniture, become the perfect choices when it

comes to small decorative pieces to place near a table light. This happens because when these materials are positioned below a light source, **they reflect the light nearby, thus creating sparkling effects that will give the room a soothing and elegant touch**. (You can also achieve a similar effect when the base of the lamp is made of metal.)

48. Another stylish option are **sculpture lamps**, meaning pieces that have an out-of-the-ordinary shape (as in the picture above) and can look like artworks when the light is turned off. To stay on the safe side, **stick to items made with just *one* material**. When lamps are made of various materials, the outcome, instead of being classy and stylish, is more like an "I-found-it-at-an-all-for-five-dollars-bazaar" effect.

49. As an additional touch to make your bedroom look more intimate, keep in mind that **lamps on side tables can be different**—and so can side tables themselves. Not only will this avoid endless arguments with your partner on the most suitable lamps for your side tables (which is already a considerable goal in itself), but it will also add a personal and cozy touch to the room.

Paintings and Mirrors

50. **Mirrors and paintings are essential elements to make a room look welcoming and considerably wider**. This is because these items, when chosen and placed in the most appropriate way, **give the eye a sensation of a longer distance**. The view goes beyond the wall, doubling the sensation of space, which makes a room appear bigger. Take advantage of it!

51. Now onto the correct positioning. As a general rule, for rooms of a regular height (about nine feet in the United States), **paintings should be placed so that their center is more or less at the same height as the eyes**, or a little higher, to achieve that sensation of "seeing beyond" described previously. Therefore, if you position a painting so that its center is at a height of about six feet from the floor (with a range of about half a foot, more or less), this usually should be suitable for most average homes (and people).

52. If the ceiling is higher than the standard, you can place the paintings in a higher position, but *only* if the room is proportionally quite wide. Conversely, **avoid placing paintings in a high position if the room is small**. This **will force the eye to look up, which gives the sensation of a smaller and unwelcoming space**.

53. Mirrors and paintings can also make a room look brighter— and here again, a correct placement is the key to achieving the desired outcome. An unsuitable position, instead of widening the space, will make the room look anything but elegant. Therefore, think twice before starting tinkering with nails and hammer. And always **take the necessary time to do several tests in different positions**, preferably with the help of your dear ones (placing paintings is always a collective activity, for the simple reason that unless you're Elastigirl, you can't hold a painting on a wall and simultaneously look at its outcome from the opposite side of the room). Not only will this **teach you, by direct experience, many interesting things about proportions and perspective**, but it's also an occasion to spend some quality time with all the family together.

54. **When in doubt, wait.** You can also **leave the painting simply leaning on the wall for some time**, until you have found its ideal placement. Besides, this practice of leaning pictures on the wall instead of hanging them is a recent trend that is undoubtedly helpful when you are on the path of making your place more stylish and welcoming. Once hung on the wall, a painting is seldom moved, even if its position is not the most appropriate. Conversely, leaving it around for some weeks (or...why not...for some months) will help you determine the best spot for it.

55. Don't forget that **paintings and mirrors must be selected considering the dimensions of the furniture they are close to**. If it goes without saying that a big painting requires a big wall, the same is valid also when it comes to the furniture near a painting. A picture to be placed over a long

dining table should be bigger than the one that you place near a little armchair. However, this rule does not apply to big paintings that cover almost the whole wall. In this case, the painting is no longer perceived as a decorative object but as a decoration of the wall itself, and it can therefore be placed near furniture of whatever dimension.

56. If you are not sure if a bigger or smaller painting is the most suitable option, choose an option in the middle and make **a composition of a few paintings** placed in line (as in the image in points number 29 and 51) or to form a rectangle or a square (as in the image below). **This is a lovely and very stylish solution that fits all spaces** since you can replicate it with a higher or lower number of paintings, depending on the dimensions of the wall itself.

57. Also, consider that you can use mirrors to cover an entire wall, regardless of the dimensions of the room. You have two options: the first one (and most expensive) is covering the entire wall with a wide mirror (this usually requires calling a

specialized worker). For a budget-friendly option, you can also **place several mirrors** in **frames that may differ in style and dimension but must be identical in color**. This solution not only is far less expensive, but it will also give the sensation of a more personal space.

58. **Don't buy pictures made with photographs taken by someone else. Do them by yourself**. Even a picture of five river stones, a detail of the flowers in your garden, or an image of an ancient floor can become wonderful and unique artwork. Just choose the appropriate colors (pictures in black and white, for instance, are always a very sophisticated option) and a beautiful frame, and you'll have something that will make your home more welcoming than ever—and, what's more important, will make you really feel at home.

59. You can also **do something similar for your kids' rooms**. Buy a dozen frames in different dimensions, then **propose that your children choose their favorite drawings and place them inside the frames**. Then hang the frames all together in the kids' rooms or in another room if you like. Not only will this make your children participate in an active way in home styling, but it will also be a **unique occasion to cultivate their good taste through direct experience**. From time to time, they can change out the old drawings with new ones. Or they can keep the artwork they made when they were three years old as something important and unique for them—and for you.

60. Regarding the color and material: when you use small frames placed all together, **white wooden frames always have a very chic effect** (of course, the wall must be any color but white). In other cases, elaborate **frames in golden or silver shades can be a very sophisticated way to add class, personality, and style** to a place where the furniture is mainly made of contemporary, minimal pieces. Conversely, **avoid frames in vivid hues, since they seldom look chic**, no matter the setting.

Fabrics

61. As a general rule, consider that **printed fabrics, even if they look stunning in themselves, are seldom the easiest choice**. This happens because printed fabrics frequently have patterns and colors that can give the impression of a messy space. They **can be used to liven up a too-clean, too-empty, perfectly organized space, but in other cases, they can be very tricky**. Therefore, if your goal is to achieve a more ordered effect, avoid prints and give preference to different shades of the same hue to spice up the room in the safest of ways.

62. However, if you like printed fabrics, **you can stay on the safe side by picking out geometric patterns or prints whose colors are in the same hue and intensity**. This will avoid the risk that the prints will make the room look messy (and also smaller). Don't forget that **it's always necessary to consider the effect of a print when seen from the other side of the room**; a pattern that can appear cute when seen closely can look dowdy (and the opposite of chic) when perceived from a distance.

63. Keep in mind that when it comes to prints, it's better to avoid trendy ones. Because they are not designed to last for a long time, their quality is frequently lower. And ironically enough, since they will stay in your house for more than just a few months, they will soon give your place an appearance that's the opposite of trendy.

64. **Perfect and very chic alternatives to printed fabrics are textured ones**. They always **pull off a sophisticated vibe, adding personality without adding clutter**, and they can therefore bring spice and class to your home without the drawbacks that printed fabrics can have. Textured fabrics, which in the past were frequently an expensive choice, **nowadays are also available in budget-friendly options but still result in high-end outcomes**. Take advantage of these options, since they are timeless choices that are always classy and trendy at the same time. Not only do textured fabrics add style and class to your place, but they also do it in a personal, sophisticated way.

65. Also, consider that **matching fabrics with different textures usually has a stylish outcome. Conversely, pairing two prints requires high style skills**. You can learn with

practice, of course, but if you want to stay on the safe side, keep it to a minimum, especially at the beginning. And start with something small and removable (such as handkerchiefs to be placed on your favorite tablecloth), instead of the cover of an armchair.

66. When it comes to throw pillows, another interesting option is **pairing cool neutral hues** (such as charcoal, gray, pearl, olive, or dusty blue, just to name a few) **with warm neutral ones** (such as oatmeal, sand, brown sugar, tan, dusty pink) as encountered in part 1 of the book. Aside from giving a polished touch to your home, this will **spice up the room in a very sophisticated and luxurious-looking way**.

67. Never cover your sofa. Sofa covers are never chic, no matter how expensive they are. They give the impression of a home that cannot be used, of a space that cannot be lived in, and of a piece that cannot be touched. And of course, this is just the opposite of chic and welcoming.

68. When it comes to **bed linens and towels**, it's essential to **find the most satisfactory brands**. Since you may find different quality standards even in the same price range, it may be wise **to invest some time in the search for brands that have higher value for the money**. You will save time, disappointment, and money for years to come. Given that you can find items with considerably different quality, even if they have approximately the same price, consider that **usually, the quality is lower for prints and colors from the most recent trends**, since we are talking about something that is not produced to last. Conversely, value for money is usually higher for brands that mainly rely on timeless hues and prints.

69. **If your bathroom has striking or out-of-the-ordinary tiles, keep the decoration of towels and bath linens to a minimum**. Rather, stick to quality items in hues that match with one of the colors of the tiles (it should not necessarily be the prevailing color; you can also achieve a stylish outcome

with towels that replicate a hue that is present in minimal quantity on the tiles).

70. Conversely, **when the tiles are quite ordinary, you can spice the bathroom up with towels in bright colors** (you can also match complementary hues if you desire).

71. You can achieve a chic and stylish outcome using **towels in tones that have the same color intensity as the tiles but a different color temperature**. For a bathroom with gray tiles, for instance (cool shade), you can use towels in the corresponding warm shade (beige or mocha, for example). In any case, however, **it's better to avoid printed towels** altogether since **they seldom look classy**.

72. **Stark white is always a timeless choice** for towels. However, **it's not the most environmentally friendly option** since it has the drawback of being chic and sophisticated only when it's sparkling, spotless, and immaculate. Don't forget this—and immediately swap any not-so-perfect item with a brand-new one. And if you want to be earth-friendly (or simply don't want to do the laundry twice a day), give preference to easier-to-manage hues.

Decorative Objects

73. **Well-chosen and well-positioned decorative objects can make the difference** between a place that's just "ordinary cute" in quite an impersonal way, and a stylish and classy home. Always consider this fact, and act with this in mind.

74. Generally, **the smaller the dimension of decorative objects** (and the bigger their number), **the higher the sensation of a messy and dowdy room**, since you can't perceive anything stylish—only a lot of undefined stuff all around.

75. Conversely, **just a few objects of medium-size dimensions** (ten to fifteen inches) **to large dimensions** (twenty to thirty

inches or more) **will make your place look chic, sophisticated, and welcoming at the same time**. Similar to our previous discussion on paintings, the dimensions of decorative objects should be chosen considering: (a) the dimension of the room—bigger items for bigger rooms, smaller items for smaller spaces, (b) the furniture: on a small side table, you will put objects that are smaller than those you will put on a big coffee table, and (c) the distance from the entrance of the room: a piece that lies far from the door should have a bigger dimension than the one you put on the shelf close to the entrance.

76. In general, as mentioned previously, **glass and metal are strategic materials for decorative objects** since they make your space look more luxurious. **Give preference to streamlined shapes and avoid items with too many details**. Neat, simple lines are always your best bets. They sound more expensive, and they require less time to remove dust and guarantee a sparkling appearance. Win-win!

77. You can **use beautiful pieces of any kind as decorative objects**. For instance, **toys, when well-made, can have outstanding results**; toy cars, rocking horses, and similar

items will add a unique and stylish touch to your place (of course, their dimension should be quite large, as mentioned earlier). Also, **books and magazines about design, architecture, travel, and art** can give a personal vibe to your home—besides, they are always pleasant to have around for a quick inspiring glance. Another option that I particularly love is placing **big bowls with fruit or vegetables** on display. **Huge vases as well are always stylish**, and you can complete them **with branches and leaves** (they are less expensive than fresh flowers and last much longer). Pieces of this kind, aside from having a personal, cozy outcome that is very pleasant, will allow you to save money and free extra space in your storage room in the bargain.

78. Interestingly, decorative objects play a role similar to that of fashion accessories. This means that they allow you to take advantage of trends that could otherwise look excessive when used for furniture. If animal prints are just all the rage, for instance, a leopard-print sofa can hardly be considered a wise choice. In contrast, a throw pillow in a leopard print can become a versatile piece to spice up a classic ensemble in a stylish way. **Well-chosen decorative objects allow you to have fun with the most recent trends in quite a safe and inexpensive way—and without the risk of looking tasteless.** Take advantage of this. Then, when the fad has passed, you can switch your leopard-print pillow covers with timeless velvet ones.

79. However, **don't throw away formerly trendy items**. Rather, store them in the storage room, or put them in beautiful storage containers. You can use them again as soon as the trend comes back—or just when your mood is set on an I-need-some-change vibe. This will make your home look different in seconds with no need to spend money on buying something new. Similarly, if you have many beautiful decorative pieces but realize that you don't have space for all of them, **make it a habit to switch out your treasures**

every few months (season changing is perfect, but you can do it any time of the year). **This will immediately make your home look new and luxurious**—even if the items in themselves are not that new indeed.

80. **Never display decorative objects that come from cheap souvenir shops.** They will **instantly downgrade even the most stylish room**.

81. Nevertheless, **trips and holidays abroad can be a useful way to buy items that you won't likely find in your neighborhood** and that can be key elements to give your place a unique, particular atmosphere. Here are some tips to guide you in these choices:

    a) Give preference to handmade objects. They won't necessarily be the most expensive options.

    b) Look for items made of natural materials such as wood, cork, leather, shells, and similar. **However, avoid those that combine more materials** since, similar to what happens to lamps (as encountered previously in point number 48), they seldom look classy.

    c) Metal also can have a very classy outcome as long as it's sparkling and has a simple pattern. Elaborate details are difficult to clean—and a dingy metal item is one of the least stylish things ever.

    d) Well-chosen artisanal fabrics can also look good, but be careful since with fabric, an appearance that's too evidently handmade is seldom chic.

82. **Place one of your most beautiful decorative objects in front of a mirror.** Its beauty will be doubled. For instance, a perfect ensemble for your entryway is a small sideboard with a table lamp on it, a stylish piece of home decor, and a mirror near them.

83. Consider that, **in small rooms, carpets frequently make the space look smaller.** Furthermore, they gather dust and

pollution, are difficult to clean, and are not the ideal choice for those with allergies. Therefore, if you live in a medium-sized apartment in a town or city, think twice before buying them since, even if they look stunning in large houses with spacious rooms, they seldom pull off the same luxurious outcome in a smaller setting.

84. Don't forget that **your most stylish bags and hats can become exclusive and chic decorative objects**! I always have some of my most beautiful handbags on display near the entrance, in the bedroom, and sometimes also in the living room. Not only will this allow you to have more space in your closet for items that cannot be displayed, but **this will also add style and identity to your place in a unique and classy way** (and on top of that, your favorite bag or most stylish hat won't risk losing their shape crushed in a corner of your closet). Additionally, **you can easily switch the pieces, making your favorite spots look different at no cost.**

85. If you would like to have something unique, an infallible (and easy) option is **creating your own contemporary artwork**. Just take a thick piece of wood (you can also use a former piece of furniture to do this) and some **acrylic decorative paint that is quite thick and dense** (ask your local DIY store for advice on the most appropriate product; you can also mix acrylic paint with sand if you want a thicker consistency), **chosen in shades that are tailored for your place.** Pour the paint over the wood and spread it with a spatula both on the surface and on the sides of the wood, molding it to obtain an irregular surface, then leave it to dry. You will have **a piece that's authentically inimitable** and, more importantly, **that's perfectly in tune with the vibe of the room and with the colors you have used in it.**

Part 4

Elevating the Everyday:

Decluttering and Space Organization

Elevating the Everyday:
Decluttering and Space Organization

86. Never skip a regular decluttering routine. Appropriate **decluttering makes any home look instantly more sophisticated**. This is the reason why so many places on the magazines and social media look high-end, even if the pieces themselves, when looked upon with a critical eye, are not that special after all. The same table, lamp, or sofa put in the very same setting would pull off a completely different outcome if it's surrounded by spare pieces that add clutter, removing identity and grace from the room. **This does not mean that everything must always be perfect**. It's rather **a matter of organization**, which mostly consists of making a habit of removing items that you realize just add confusion from visible spots. I know that sometimes we are too tired, too busy, or simply involved in other thoughts to consider decluttering, but **if you keep things easy and pleasant**—for instance, **turning on your favorite music** or **switching on soothing, relaxing lights** during your decluttering sessions—**it will become a regular, quick, and enjoyable habit**, and things will flow automatically.

87. Frequently, when it comes to decluttering and reorganizing things and places, we don't know where to start. Speaking from personal experience, I found that **a simple, effective, and even fun way to declutter consists of sorting by color every piece that is in a given room** *(including the smallest items in particular)*, **then removing all the objects that have**

hues that just don't go with the main ones. Don't think that something small is not important or that it cannot even be perceived; frequently, the truth is exactly the opposite. Sure, **apparently insignificant pieces that are out of place**, or that are not in tune with the main vibe of the place, **are hardly perceived *directly*. However, they are perceived *unconsciously*, which is far worse**, since they transmit a general impression of disorder that cannot be attributed to anything particular, and therefore may be harder to change. So roll up your sleeves and go in search of that small fuchsia sewing thread roll that you left on your light-blue sofa after fixing a button on your daughter's favorite shorts. **You will be amazed at how more streamlined and how much neater your home will immediately look**.

88. Change your mind, change your places: trying to **reconsider the position of what lies on the shelves, on the cupboard**, on the coffee table, and maybe also inside your closet, pantry,

or drawers, is **an interesting and alternative way to declutter**. Things are not always in the most appropriate place to be used (and found) where you need them. By the way, this is an extra tip that will be very useful if you're inclined to pass half of your time looking for some lost item, because **the foolproof trick to identify the most perfect location for everything is putting things *in the first place* you've looked for them** when you weren't able to find them anywhere. You've lost hours looking for that evening clutch that you don't often use, haven't you? Well, as soon as you can find your vanished item, immediately put that article in the first place you tried to find it, and always keep it there, because that's exactly where you'll go hunting for it next time!

89. **For small to medium pieces that you need to keep at hand** in your living room or bedroom (such as the TV remote control, your favorite coasters, the nail file, notepads, eyeglasses, battery chargers, and all of those wires that you use from time to time), a lovely and convenient option is **putting them into a beautiful box with a lid** to keep in view. The boxes can be in faux leather, for instance, or velvet, or any other lovely material, as long as it's a solid color (printed items are not even to be considered since they would only add clutter instead of lessening it). This way, they can become almost part of the furniture. I use nice-looking storage containers with covers also for those items that I usually need just before leaving home, such as foldable umbrellas, hats, gloves, and so on.

90. **For your bathroom and kitchen, you can use old shoeboxes** without covers to be kept inside the cabinets to store spare objects that otherwise would not have a regular place. They will become **sort of hidden (and totally inexpensive) drawers that will allow more efficient use of space** and that—unlike drawers—you can easily remove from their position whenever you need to search for something with ease.

91. **When it comes to bigger pieces**, consider that, even if they may look out of place in a given setting (or not consistent regarding colors or materials), **it can be enough to move them to another position to achieve a completely different—and much more sophisticated—effect**. Sometimes, even the simple fact of placing something in a position that's close to a lamp can pull off an entirely different outcome. Explore new options, do some tests, and make the find-my-perfect-place experience into a fun game!

92. As I already mentioned in one of my previous books, the most effective decluttering strategy can be found in the novel *The Little Prince*, by Antoine de Saint-Exupéry: "Perfection is achieved not when there is nothing more to add, but when there is nothing left to take away." **Removing unnecessary stuff from your settings** not only **will instantly make it look more stylish and sophisticated**, but it will also give you (and those who live with you) a positive sensation of energy. **You will feel relaxed and fulfilled instead of just feeling overwhelmed** by what you have around you. And on

top of that, the lovely things you have will sparkle instead of being concealed in a sea of superfluous stuff.

93. Think twice (at least) before buying something new—and I'm not writing this just as a figure of speech! If you make it a habit to **never buy something right away but only after at least a day has passed** (unless you have just landed at the North Pole to find out that the airline delivered you the baggage of a passenger that was clearly headed to Hawaii), not only will you frequently save money, but **you won't have a home chock-full of stuff that is not, after all, that necessary**. Years ago, I decided to make it a habit to purchase something only after the second time (at least) I saw it, and I try to stick to this resolution whenever it is possible. Frequently, I get out of a shop without purchasing the chosen item, and before buying it, I go home and check if it goes well with some of the garments I already have (if it's a garment); if I can find space for it (if it's a tool for the kitchen); and if I don't already have something very similar (in all cases).

Sometimes I come back and make my purchase. Sometimes I don't. In the first case, I know that I've found something I'm really glad about. In the second case, I'm still glad that I did not waste money and space on something that would just add clutter to the home. This is valid also for online purchases, where things are even easier since you don't need to take your car and drive for miles to make purchases.

94. **Always start a decluttering session with something small.** If you began with the biggest walk-in you have, things could easily take a time considerably longer than expected—and neither the most inveterate declutter-addicted person wants to sleep on a bed entirely covered with winter coats and padded jackets (especially if it's the fifteenth of August). Therefore, you'll swear to yourself that you won't even consider decluttering for the next ten years—if ever. Conversely, starting from a shelf in your bathroom will guarantee lovely and fulfilling results, which means that **you will quickly want to extend your newly achieved decluttering skills to all you have around**, with no worries that things could become overwhelming.

95. Make it a habit to **get rid of at least one unused item every time you buy something new**. This is a very effective trick that not only will prevent your home from becoming overflowing with useless things, but also (if you get used to always doing so) will enable you to **avoid unwise purchases**. Before buying your twentieth black sweater, for instance, have a look at what you already have in your closet. Get rid of that one that lost its shape (or color), or that does not have a perfect fit for your figure; no matter their price, garments of this kind will never make you look chic. And maybe you will come across a brand-new piece that you bought at the end of the past season, which you had entirely forgotten.

96. I know, sometimes we are somehow reluctant to get rid of stuff that's still almost new or that could prove to be useful one day or another...who knows? A lovely solution to breaking this deadlock lies in **giving the too-good-to-go item to a dear friend that you know will appreciate it.** And

if she or he is really a dear friend, you can also agree that should you ever have any second thoughts about your "gift," you can immediately have it back. Speaking from personal experience, every time I give something to my cousin (and coauthor) Benedetta or to my mother, I always have them swear on their own life that they are going to give it back to me right away as soon as I realize that I need it. Which of course, so far has never happened.

97. Going in search of things that you don't use anymore but that can be appreciated by friends and family, aside from being useful, can also become a fun game to play with your dear ones on a rainy Sunday afternoon. Try it! I bet you'll like it.

98. When it comes to clothes managing, we are all aware that **a closet overflowing with clothes and accessories** not only does *not* guarantee that you always pick out the perfect outfit for your day, but also **drains your energy**, because you may

easily **get lost in a sea of garments that don't call your name, making you forget those that can make you shine**. In contrast, the right amount of well-chosen, well-organized clothing will allow you to always look chic, stylish, and sophisticated. Easier said than done, I know. **Sometimes, we just can't figure out what's worth keeping** and what we should get rid of. To achieve this target with ease, it may be useful **to take pictures (also—and especially—from the rear side) of items you're uncertain about** since this will allow you to perceive their real outcome. You may also **use pictures to keep in mind ensembles that you love**, as in the figure below; this will be very helpful when you are on one of those I-have-nothing-to-wear days, since being aware that you have chic and flattering outfits available will prevent you from making unwise purchases. Also, seeing garments together will help you figure out their outcome and help you get rid of the items that don't go with anything.

Another option is **asking a dear friend to help (and support!) you in the selection**. (And if you want to better understand the key guidelines for a proper choice, you may also have a look at my style manuals *Wardrobe Essentials for a Woman of Charme* and *Flattering Fashion*, where you will find the main directions and visual examples to pick out your perfect baseline staples as well as those trendy pieces that will make your outfit look unique).

99. Raise your hand if you have ever found a lovely garment relegated in a hidden corner of your drawers—even though it was just the thing you were looking for when planning a special evening. **Having well-organized drawers is not easy.** Frequently we use them to store things randomly without even realizing what we are putting inside them. Here again, to make things flow better, **it can be helpful to use old shoeboxes that will allow you to better separate the contents of a drawer** (and when you do the seasonal restock, you can simply store the boxes with all their contents on the highest shelves with no need to empty them).

100. Also, consider that a useful trick to have a more orderly wardrobe while, at the same time, making the outfit selection process more successful lies in **arranging your clothes by color** (if your wardrobe contains pieces of many different hues) **or by shade** (light or dark) if your closet mainly consists of staple neutral shades. Aside from being useful, making your choice easier, items organized by color are so nice to see, and **this simple change will automatically make your closet look more orderly**, with an **immediate I-have-made-a-big-decluttering visual effect**—even if you did not get rid of any item, indeed.

101. To conclude, here is **a final trick that combines decluttering with styling**. Do you have something (a piece of furniture, a chest of drawers, a decorative object) that you love, but you realize it's not the most appropriate color for the room you placed it in? Take paint and brush and **change its color** (you can also use the distressing technique described in point number 41). It's easier than it seems,

believe me. **The space will immediately look more ordered and well-organized, and the room will look more sophisticated.**

Hooray!

Conclusion

In this little manual, you've found the staple guidelines to turn your place into your dream home by following a few easy steps that will allow you to achieve your target with ease.

What's important, now, is going on with doing a good job, to create **a home that will be more beautiful and pleasant to live in every day**—a home where you can find time and space for yourself, and a welcoming place that you can enjoy with family and friends.

To do so, a couple of recommendations may be useful:

- Make it a habit to **write down in a small notebook a list of medium- to long-term targets for your home**. It may be something as simple as buying new coat hangers for your closet or decluttering a couple of shelves in your pantry, as well as bigger tasks such as repainting your kids' desks or buying a new sofa. This will help you **focus on your goals and achieve the desired outcome more easily**—even if you are still taking the necessary time to make the most suitable choices.

- Your little list will also give you a line to follow when window-shopping or simply strolling around. **Everything around you can become inspiring.** If you have clear targets in mind, things will flow on autopilot—and making choices that will allow you to successfully achieve your goals will become innate.

Always keep in mind that creating your dream home is all about **merging practical with aesthetic goals**, as you've learned in these pages. This is the key to achieving outstanding results since a space that's well-organized and beautiful at the same time is a space where everything can flow better.

Also, consider that, as mentioned at the beginning of the book, **living in a lovely, charming, and enjoyable setting** not only is **a powerful tool to feel in a positive mood and to improve your familial relationships**, but it will also boost your self-esteem, allowing you to feel (and become) more successful in many areas of your life in the bargain.

As I have explained in detail in my manual *101 Ways to Become Your Best Chic Self*, when all around you is chaotic, it can be hard to feel chic—let alone successful. Conversely, **if you elevate the quality of your setting**, if you live in a place that's pleasant, stylish, and easy to handle, not only will this make you feel more polished and fulfilled, but **it will also make you feel more successful**.

Living in a chic setting impacts your mindset, **giving start to a virtuous circle that can boost positive vibes and a successful mood**. It's a circular process that, once started, will flow almost automatically.

When you are surrounded by beauty, **your mind will unconsciously perceive that you *deserve* that beauty**. That you deserve to live in a chic, sophisticated place. **That you are worth having a classy, stylish setting around you**.

All these sensations will **instinctively channel your most successful self**, encouraging you to showcase your best qualities.

You will instantly feel positive sensations of energy.

And you will soon realize how your newly achieved chic home will **boost your mood and increase your self-confidence**, enhancing successful vibes and allowing you to **truly feel and become, more and more every day, the best and chicest version of yourself**.

About the Author

Chiara Giuliani is an architect and fashion writer based in Florence, Italy, and author of several popular books about fashion and lifestyle. After being published in academic and professional publications, in 2012, she wrote her first style manual, *La casa di charme*, a guide for making your home your own unique place with tips to make spaces look visually bigger and more proportional. In 2016, she published her second book, *La Donna di Charme* (English title: *How to Become a Woman of* Charme), a manual of personal style meant to help women of all ages and body types feel more beautiful while boosting their self-confidence. In collaboration with her cousin Benedetta Belloni, who worked for years in the field of custom luxury garments, she founded the website *ladonnadicharme.com* where she shares priceless tips to identify the most flattering trends and to achieve a chic and figure-enhancing look. In 2017, she published the manual *101 Ways to Look Slimmer and Taller*, followed by the books *Wardrobe Essentials for a Woman of* Charme (2018), *101 Ways to Look Expensive on a Budget* (2019), *Flattering Fashion* (2021), *The Fashion Diet*, and *101 Ways to Become Your Best Chic Self*, which contain practical suggestions to stretch out the silhouette in a stylish way with the help of a smart choice of clothing pieces and with the support of an appropriate lifestyle. In the mini-book you're now holding, Chiara is back on her architectural roots; you will find, streamlined for you, practical and easy-to-follow hints and visual tricks to create your dream home, thus achieving a place that's chic, stylish, easier to manage, and that's in tune with the chic and charming lady that you already are.

Style and Class Are Architecture.
They Are a Matter of Proportion.

www.ladonnadicharme.com

When you are surrounded by beauty,
your mind will unconsciously perceive
that you deserve that beauty.
That you deserve to live in a chic, sophisticated place.

This will instinctively channel
your most successful self.

And you will soon realize
how your newly achieved chic home
will boost your mood and increase your self-confidence,
allowing you to feel and become
the best and chicest version of yourself.

Made in the USA
Coppell, TX
28 August 2025

53972918R10046